Character Queen's ABC's

I am the Character Queen
and I want you to do the right thing!
Someone else wants you to do right, too!
That's why this book was chosen **JUST FOR YOU**!

The ABC's were given to

_____

by

_____

on

_____
(Date)

Copyright 2015 by Little Rock Life Skillz

All rights reserved. No part of this book may be reproduced, stored in a retrieval system, or transmitted in any form by any means: electronic, mechanical, photo-copying, recording, or otherwise without prior written permission except in the case of the brief quotations embodied in critical articles and reviews. Inquiries and requests are to be sent to: mona@characterqueensabcs.com.

First Edition
Printed in the United States of America

Character Queen's ABC's
By Raymona L. Ellison

ISBN 978-0-692-57482-9

children . family . guidebook . self-help . education . poetry

Art by
Anthony "y,not" Williams

Cover design and book layout and design by
Kennesha M. Walker of Miwa Design and Graphics

Inquiries, please email: mona@characterqueensabcs.com
or visit our website at www.characterqueensabcs.com

This book
is dedicated to
our 5 Princesses
and Langston

"Good character is not innate. It is learned."

-Donna Brown, MD (ABPN Board Certified Psychiatrist)

"It is important that children feel cared for and also learn to care for others. The Character Queen program has taught Michaela to properly engage and interact with her teachers, fellow students, family, and friends. You have left a lifetime impression on her and I am forever grateful."

-Suzanne Williams (Character Queen Program Parent)

"This book is a must-have for teaching and learning character at an early age. Learning character early in life makes for a more responsible adulthood."

-Ms. Rosie Coleman (Executive Director of Elementary Education
North Little Rock School District)

"I have worked with all ages of kids for over 45 years in hospitals, counseling centers, and prisons, delivering mental health services. Many of them would not have needed those services if they had been given appropriate character education at an early age."

- Larry P. Henderson, DMin, LPC-S, LMFT-S, CCDP-D

"What better way to raise selfless children than to help them to see how kindness, honesty and sharing are important in building community."

- Bruce Morgan
CEO, Kids Across America Kamps

Character Queen's ABC's

by
Raymona L. Ellison
Illustrated by
Anthony Williams

www.characterqueensabcs.com

It may be scary,
but I can say:
I can face it,
for I am **BRAVE**!

I'll keep going!
I'll keep trying!
I know I can win!
I'm **DETERMINED**
to do my best
until the very end!

If I tell you, "You can do it," you believe it's true! I believe you can do it. I'll **ENCOURAGE** you!

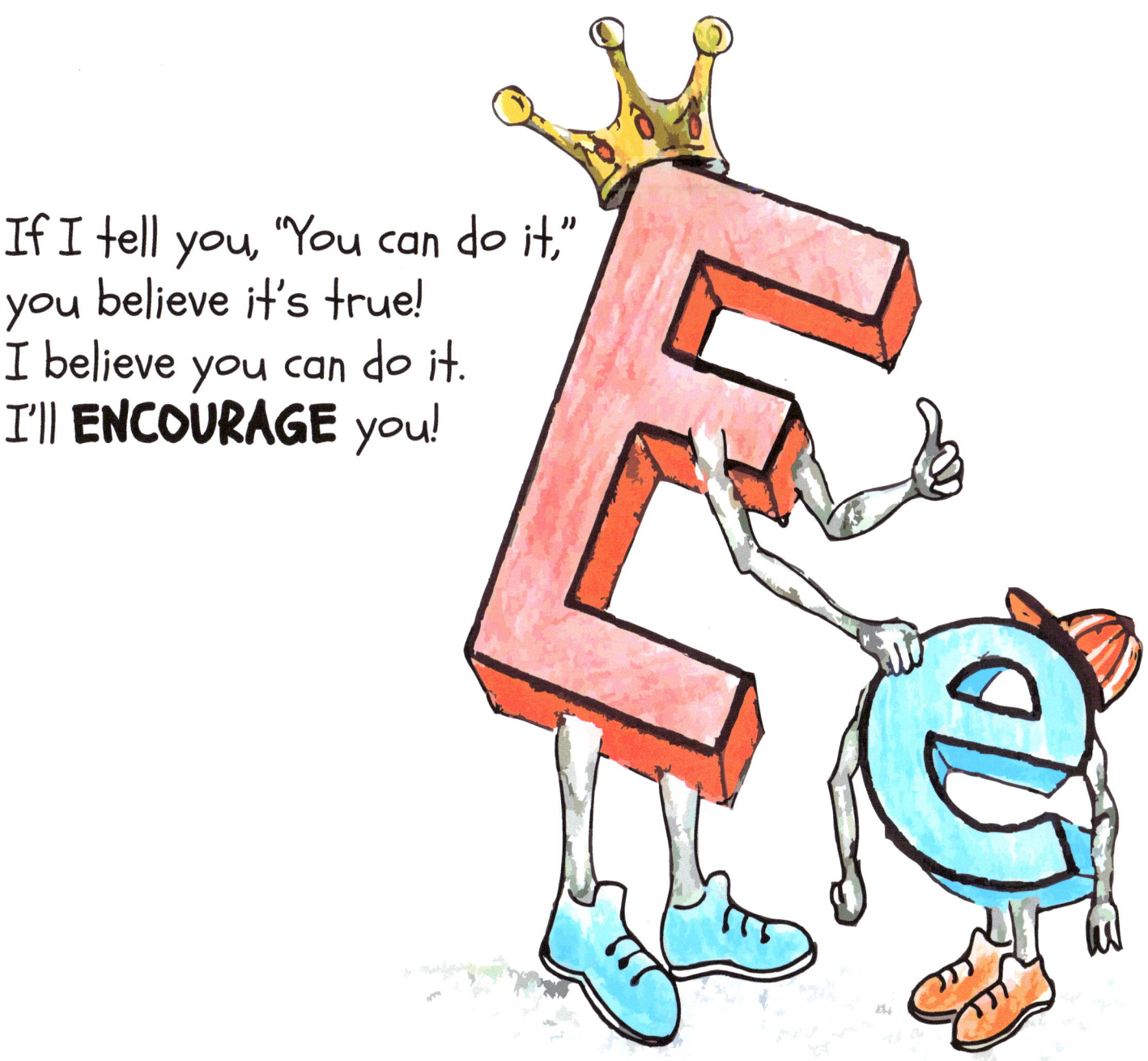

If I want one, I must be one,
I know this is true.
I'll be kind – encouraging, too!
I'll be a **FRIEND** to you!

Clothes to wear;
Food to eat;
A family to love –
I'm **GRATEFUL** as can be!

I will not lie, cheat, nor steal.
You can count on me.
I will always tell the truth.
I'm **HONEST** as can be!

I am smart and I am strong.
I can do it on my own.
INDEPENDENT! That is me!
I'll do it by myself. You'll see!

See this smile upon my face?
I am filled with glee!
JOYFUL! **JOYFUL!** I am **JOYFUL!!**
I'm happy as can be!

How can I be
KIND to you??
Be considerate, helpful,
and thoughtful too!

I'm **LOYAL** to you, you're **LOYAL** to me – committed to each other like family!

I use good **MANNERS** –
a respectful tool.
"Please" and "Thank You" –
that's the rule!

I keep it tidy.
I keep it clean.
I am **NEAT**!
You know what I mean?!

When things look bad, find a reason to be glad! That's called **OPTIMISM!**

PERSEVERANCE! Keep on trying!
PERSEVERANCE! Never stop!
PERSEVERANCE! I can do it!
PERSEVERANCE! Reach the top!

There are times I can
be noisy and loud –
outside and having fun!
But there are also times I
need to turn down,
be **QUIET**, and get things done.

R-E-S-P-E-C-T! I know what it means to me!
I'll treat you the way I want you to treat me.
R-E-S-P-E-C-T!

There's no need to wonder.
I'll say just what I feel.
I'll be **SINCERE** – speak from my heart
and always keep it real.

If I say it, I will do it.
You can count on me!
I am honest. I'll keep my promise.
I am **TRUSTWORTHY**!

I am aware of what you feel.
I am forgiving, too.
I UNDERSTAND: we all mess up!
And I'll still be kind to you.

I don't just think about today.
I am a **VISIONARY**.
I consider my future, too.
I'll be great! You'll see!

I can use good judgment.
I can use **WISDOM**, too.
It doesn't always come with age –
just knowing the right thing to do.

I'll be **XENIAL** towards you
and greet you with good cheer!
Welcome to this place I love!
I'm so glad you're here!

Character List

A is for ADAPTABILITY
B is for BRAVE
C is for COMPASSION
D is for DETERMINED
E is for ENCOURAGING
F is for FRIENDLY
G is for GRATEFUL
H is for HONEST
I is for INDEPENDENT
J is for JOYFUL
K is for KIND
L is for LOYAL
M is for MANNERED

N is for NEAT
O is for OPTIMISM
P is for PERSEVERANCE
Q is for QUIET
R is for RESPECT
S is for SINCERE
T is for TRUSTWORTHY
U is for UNDERSTANDING
V is for VISIONARY
W is for WISDOM
X is for XENIAL
Y is for YOUTHFUL
Z is for ZEALOUS

About the Author

One of Raymona's greatest motivations is to help young people make good choices for their lives. From directing Youth Programs at Love Truth Care Ministries (serving kids in the historic Central High School neighborhood) to directing Children's Ministries at Saint Mark Baptist Church – her passion is to sow into the lives of kids as they grow into their purpose. She now leads Little Rock Life Skillz (since 2013). The organization teaches high school students to make healthy choices in their relationships, and character education to young children through the Character Queen program.

Raymona lives in Little Rock with her husband, Gary. They have 5 daughters, and the cutest grandboy ever!